Published by Sellers Publishing, Inc.
161 John Roberts Road, South Portland, Maine 04106
Visit our Web site: www.sellerspublishing.com • E-mail: rsp@rsvp.com

Copyright © 2015 Sellers Publishing, Inc.
Illustrations copyright © 2015 Robin Pickens
All rights reserved.

Compiled by Robin Haywood

ISBN 13: 978-1-4162-4571-1

10 9 8 7 6 5 4 3 2 1

Printed and bound in China.

Seize the Day

the Day

Inspiring Words for the Journey Ahead

Art & Design by ROBIN PICKENS

SELLERS
PUBLISHING

Begin

Each day
unfolds with
fresh new
potential.

Robin Pickens

It is better to be prepared
for an opportunity
and not have one
than to have an
opportunity and
not be prepared.

Whitney M. Young

6

Ready

Fortune

There never is but one opportunity of a kind.

Henry David Thoreau

Genius is
1 percent
inspiration
and 99 percent
perspiration.

Thomas Edison

Original

Dedication

In the confrontation between
the stream and the rock, the stream
always wins — not through
strength but by perseverance.

H. Jackson Browne Jr.

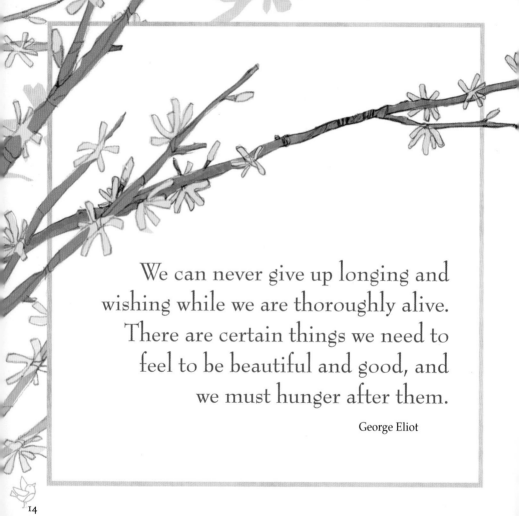

We can never give up longing and wishing while we are thoroughly alive. There are certain things we need to feel to be beautiful and good, and we must hunger after them.

George Eliot

Yearn

Observant

Opportunity is
missed by most people
because it is dressed
in overalls and
looks like work.

Thomas Edison

17

When obstacles arise,
you change your direction
to reach your goal,
you do not change your
decision to get there.

Zig Ziglar

Adapt

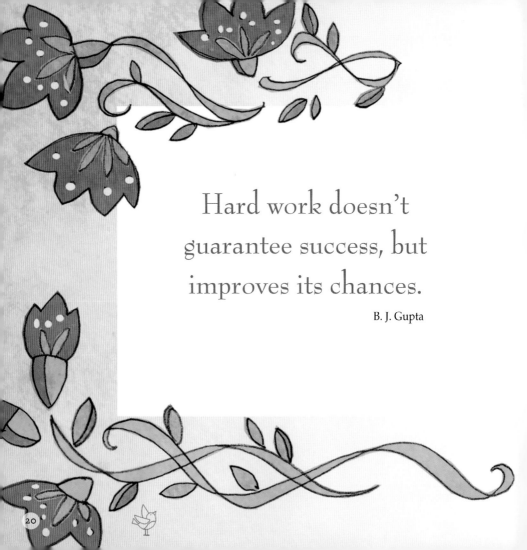

Hard work doesn't guarantee success, but improves its chances.

B. J. Gupta

Commitment

Purpose

You've got to get up every morning
with determination if you're going
to go to bed with satisfaction.

George Horace Lorimer

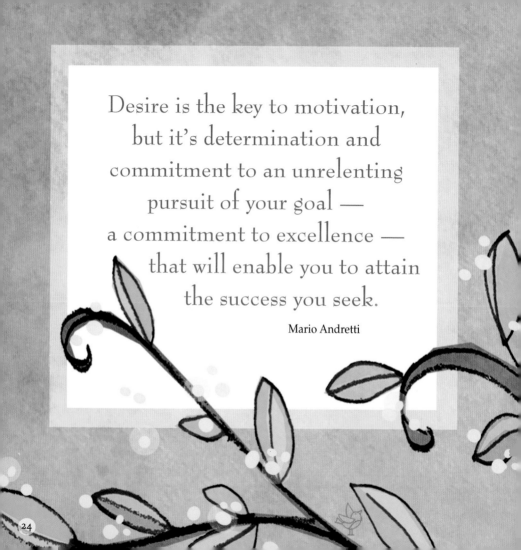

Desire is the key to motivation,
but it's determination and
commitment to an unrelenting
pursuit of your goal —
a commitment to excellence —
that will enable you to attain
the success you seek.

Mario Andretti

Resolve

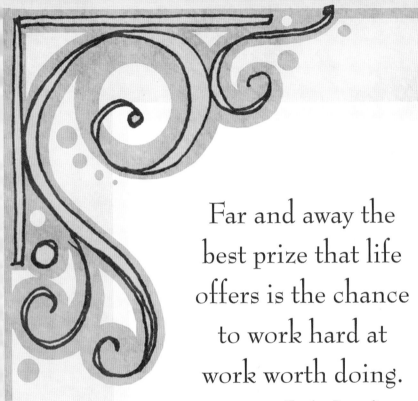

Far and away the
best prize that life
offers is the chance
to work hard at
work worth doing.

Theodore Roosevelt

Every day is filled with
exploration and
the chance to
discover something
wonderful.

Robin Pickens

Uncover

Revelation

Little gifts of discovery await you today.

Robin Pickens

Discover a new part of you.
Try a different approach, a lighter attitude,
a fresh outlook. Every day is a chance
to reinvent yourself.

Robin Pickens

Delight

Courage

Don't let the fear of
striking out hold you back.

Babe Ruth

Experience is
a hard teacher
because she gives
the test first,
the lesson
afterwards.

Vernon Sanders Law

Learn

Knowledge

Nothing is a waste
of time if you use
the experience wisely.

Auguste Rodin

Do not let making
a living prevent you
from making a life.

John Wooden

Happiness

Don't wait until everything is just right.
It will never be perfect. There will always be
challenges, obstacles, and less-than-perfect
conditions. So what. Get started now. With
each step you take, you will grow stronger
and stronger, more and more skilled, more
and more self-confident, and more and
more successful.

Mark Victor Hansen

Defeat should never be a source of discouragement, but rather a fresh stimulus.

Bishop Robert South

Encouragement

Your assumptions are your windows on the world. Scrub them off every once in a while, or the light won't come in.

Alan Alda

Reawaken

Magic

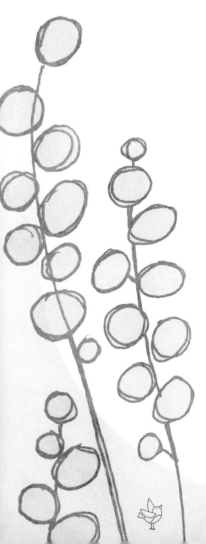

Somewhere,
something
incredible is
waiting to
be known.

Dr. Carl Sagan

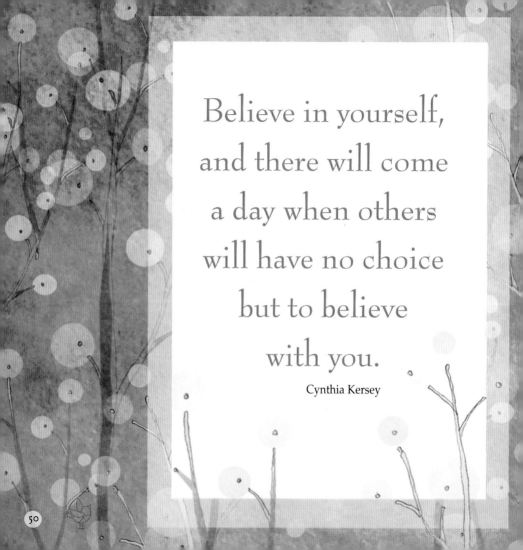

Believe in yourself,
and there will come
a day when others
will have no choice
but to believe
with you.

Cynthia Kersey

Confidence

Believe

The height of your
accomplishments will
equal the depth of
your convictions.

William F. Scolavino

53

Someone with their feet planted firmly on the ground has no hope of reaching the stars.

Kelsey Dunn

54

Reach

Pursue

Follow your passion,
listen to your heart,
make every day a celebration
of your vision and soul.

Robin Pickens

Be bold!
Shine with
all your
color and
character.

Robin Pickens

58

Aspire to

Realize

We are each
gifted in a unique
and important way.
It is our privilege and
our adventure to
discover our own
special light.

Mary Dunbar

61

Fly high.
Be brilliant.
Celebrate all your
accomplishments.

Robin Pickens

Celebrate

Kindness

Be aware of what others are doing,
applaud their efforts, acknowledge
their successes, and encourage them
in their pursuits. When we all help
one another, everybody wins.

Jim Stovall

It takes courage to grow up and become who you really are.

E. E. Cummings

Become

Determination

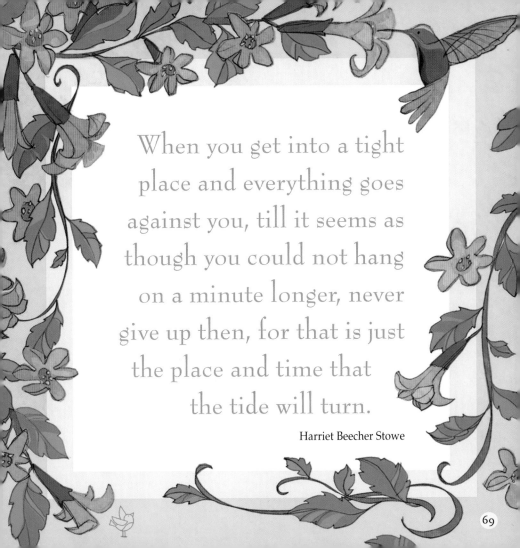

When you get into a tight place and everything goes against you, till it seems as though you could not hang on a minute longer, never give up then, for that is just the place and time that the tide will turn.

Harriet Beecher Stowe

Be what you are.
This is the first step
toward becoming
better than you are.

Julius Charles Hare

Honesty

Awaken

I've come to believe that each of us has a personal calling that's as unique as a fingerprint — and that the best way to succeed is to discover what you love and then find a way to offer it to others in the form of service, working hard, and also allowing the energy of the universe to lead you.

Oprah Winfrey

Confident

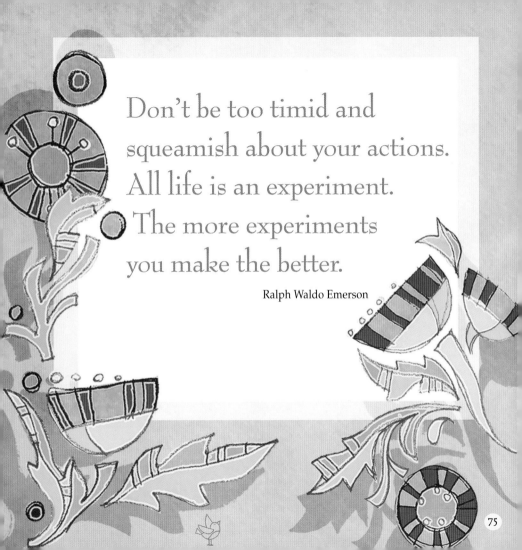

Don't be too timid and squeamish about your actions. All life is an experiment. The more experiments you make the better.

Ralph Waldo Emerson

To fulfill a dream,
to be allowed to sweat
over lonely labor,
to be given the chance
to create — that is
the meat and potatoes
of life. The money
is the gravy. As everyone else,
I love to dunk my crust in it. But
alone, it is not a diet designed
to keep body and soul together.

Bette Davis

Passion

Strength

People grow through experience if they meet life honestly and courageously. This is how character is built.

Eleanor Roosevelt

Advice is what we ask
for when we already
know the answer
but wish we didn't.

Erica Jong

Knowing

Grow

The thing that is really hard, and really amazing, is giving up on being perfect and beginning the work of becoming yourself.

Anna Quindlen

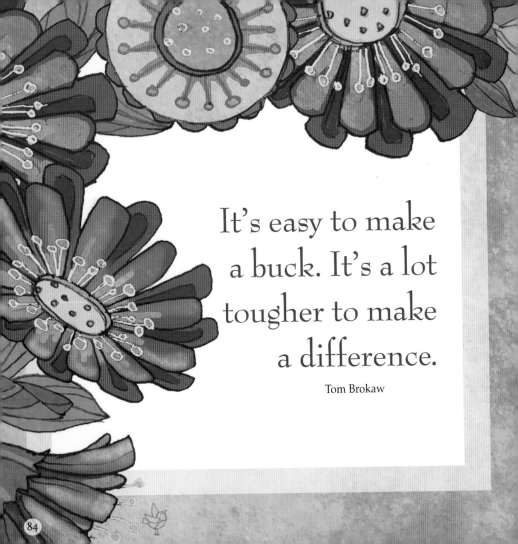

It's easy to make a buck. It's a lot tougher to make a difference.

Tom Brokaw

Seek

Courage

Wherever you go,
go with all
your heart.

Confucius

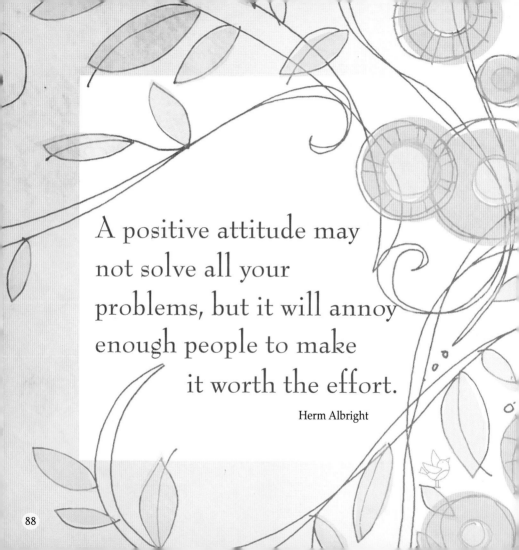

A positive attitude may not solve all your problems, but it will annoy enough people to make it worth the effort.

Herm Albright

Smile

Benevolent

The habit of being uniformly considerate toward others will bring increased happiness to you.

Grenville Kleiser

If you don't try at
anything, you can't fail
. . . it takes backbone
to lead the life
you want.

Richard Yates

Tenacity

Dream

Sometimes
I've believed as
many as six
impossible things
before breakfast.

Lewis Carroll

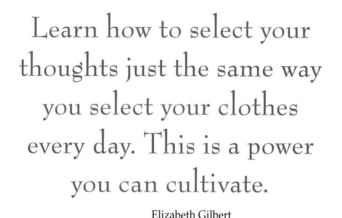

Learn how to select your thoughts just the same way you select your clothes every day. This is a power you can cultivate.

Elizabeth Gilbert

Manage

Daring

Beware;
for I am fearless.
And therefore
powerful.

Mary Shelley

Our workaday lives are filled with
opportunities to bless others.
The power of a single glance or
an encouraging smile must
never be underestimated.

G. Richard Rieger

Acknowledge

Triumph

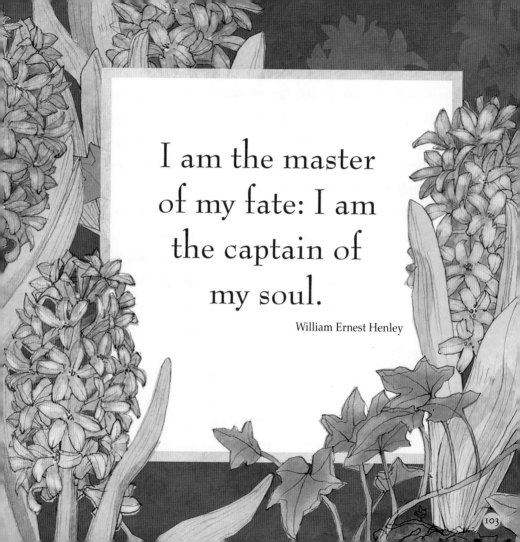

I am the master of my fate: I am the captain of my soul.

William Ernest Henley

The grand essentials of happiness are: something to do, something to love, and something to hope for.

Allan K. Chalmers

Necessary

Experience

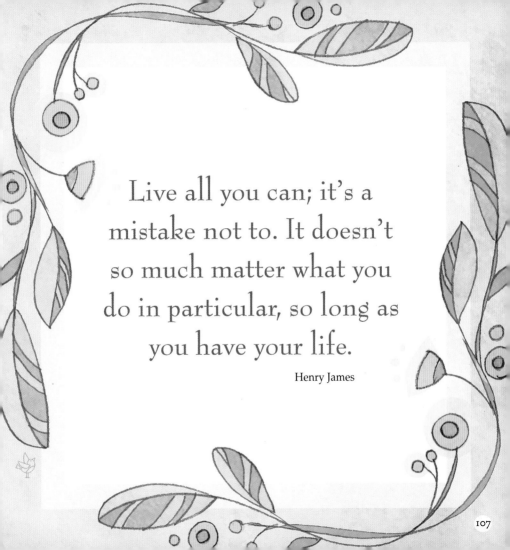

Live all you can; it's a
mistake not to. It doesn't
so much matter what you
do in particular, so long as
you have your life.

Henry James

There's only one real sin, and that is to persuade oneself that the second-best is anything but the second-best.

Doris Lessing

Truth

Insight

Don't try to comprehend with your mind. Your minds are very limited. Use your intuition.

Madeleine L'Engel

Nurture your mind with great thoughts. To believe in the heroic makes heroes.

Benjamin Disraeli

Attention

Live

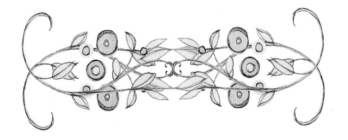

It does not do to
dwell on dreams
and forget to live,
remember that.

J. K. Rowling

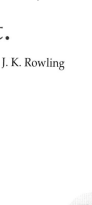

Cherish your friends, stay true to your principles, live passionately and fully and well. Experience new things. Love and be loved, if you ever get the chance.

David Nicholls

Conscious

Fierce

...[I]f you are interested in something,
no matter what it is, go at it at full speed
ahead. Embrace it with both arms, hug it,
love it, and above all become passionate about it.
Lukewarm is no good. Hot is no good either.
White hot and passionate
is the only thing to be.

Roald Dahl

Things do
not change;
we change.

Henry David Thoreau

Fact

Aim

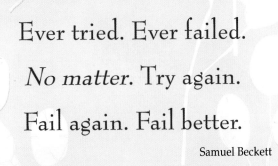

Ever tried. Ever failed.

No matter. Try again.

Fail again. Fail better.

Samuel Beckett

Do one thing
every day
that scares

you.

Eleanor Roosevelt

Gutsy

Mature

You have to do your
own growing no matter how
tall your grandfather was.

Abraham Lincoln